new interchange

Jack C. Richards

*video
activity
book*

1

CAMBRIDGE
UNIVERSITY PRESS

Revised for use with *New Interchange*

PUBLISHED BY THE PRESS SYNDICATE OF THE UNIVERSITY OF CAMBRIDGE
The Pitt Building, Trumpington Street, Cambridge, United Kingdom

CAMBRIDGE UNIVERSITY PRESS
The Edinburgh Building, Cambridge CB2 2RU, UK http://www.cup.cam.ac.uk
40 West 20th Street, New York, NY 10011–4211, USA http://www.cup.org
10 Stamford Road, Oakleigh, Melbourne 3166, Australia
Ruiz de Alarcón 13, 28014 Madrid, Spain

© Cambridge University Press 1994, 1997

First published 1994
Second edition 1997
Fourth printing 2000

Printed in the United States of America
Typeset in Century Schoolbook

ISBN 0 521 62881 4 Student's Book 1
ISBN 0 521 62880 6 Student's Book 1A
ISBN 0 521 62879 2 Student's Book 1B
ISBN 0 521 62878 4 Workbook 1
ISBN 0 521 62877 6 Workbook 1A
ISBN 0 521 62876 8 Workbook 1B
ISBN 0 521 62875 X Teacher's Edition 1
ISBN 0 521 62874 1 Teacher's Manual 1
ISBN 0 521 62873 3 Class Audio Cassettes 1
ISBN 0 521 62871 7 Student's Audio Cassette 1A
ISBN 0 521 62869 5 Student's Audio Cassette 1B
ISBN 0 521 62872 5 Class Audio CDs 1
ISBN 0 521 62870 9 Student's Audio CD 1A
ISBN 0 521 62868 7 Student's Audio CD 1B
ISBN 0 521 62867 9 Video 1 (NTSC)

ISBN 0 521 62866 0 Video 1 (PAL)
ISBN 0 521 62865 2 Video 1 (SECAM)
ISBN 0 521 62864 4 Video Activity Book 1
ISBN 0 521 62863 6 Video Teacher's Guide 1
ISBN 0 521 62667 6 CD-ROM (PC format)
ISBN 0 521 62666 8 CD-ROM (Mac format)

Available from the First Edition
ISBN 0 521 46759 4 Placement Test
ISBN 0 521 42217 5 Lab Cassette Set 1
ISBN 0 521 42218 3 Lab Guide 1

Available in 2000
ISBN 0 521 62882 2 Placement Test (revised)

Book design, art direction, and layout services: Adventure House, NYC
Illustrators: Adventure House, Brian Battles, Keith Bendis, Mark Kaufman,
  Wally Neibart, Andrew Toos, Sam Viviano

Plan of Video Activity Book 1

Introduction

NEW INTERCHANGE

New Interchange is a revision of *Interchange,* one of the world's most successful and popular English courses. *New Interchange* is a multi-level course in English as a second or foreign language for young adults and adults. The course covers the four skills of listening, speaking, reading, and writing, as well as improving pronunciation and building vocabulary. Particular emphasis is placed on listening and speaking. The primary goal of the course is to teach communicative competence, that is, the ability to communicate in English according to the situation, purpose, and roles of the participants. The language used in *New Interchange* is American English; however, the course reflects the fact that English is the major language of international communication and is not limited to any one country, region, or culture. Level One is for students at the beginner or false-beginner level.

Level One builds on the foundations for accurate and fluent communication already established in the *Intro* Level by extending grammatical, lexical, and functional skills. The syllabus covered in Level One also incorporates a rapid review of language from the *Intro* Level, allowing Student's Book 1 to be used with students who have not studied with *Intro*.

THE VIDEO COURSE

New Interchange Video 1 has been revised for use with *New Interchange*. The Video is designed to complement the Student's Book or to be used independently as the basis for a short listening and speaking course.

As a complement to the Student's Book, the Video provides a variety of entertaining and instructive live-action sequences. Each video sequence provides further practice related to the topics, language, and vocabulary introduced in the corresponding unit of the Student's Book.

As the basis for a short, free-standing course, the Video serves as an exciting vehicle for intro-ducing and practicing useful conversational language used in everyday situations.

The Video Activity Book contains a wealth of activities that reinforce and extend the content of the Video, whether it is used to supplement the Student's Book or as the basis for an independent course. The Video Teacher's Guide provides thorough support for both situations.

COURSE LENGTH

The Video contains sixteen dramatized sequences and five documentary sequences. These vary slightly in length, but in general, the sequences are approximately three minutes each, and the documentaries are approximately five minutes each.

The accompanying units in the Video Activity Book are designed for maximum flexibility and provide anywhere from 45 to 90 minutes of classroom activity. Optional activities described in the Video Teacher's Guide may be used to extend the lesson as needed.

MORE ABOUT THE COURSE COMPONENTS

Video

The sixteen video sequences complement Units 1 through 16 of *New Interchange* Student's Book 1. Although each sequence is linked to the topic of the corresponding Student's Book unit, it presents a new situation and introduces characters who do not appear in the text. This element of diversity helps keep students' interest high and also allows the Video to be used effectively as a free-standing course. At the same time, the language used in the video sequences reflects the structures and vocabulary of the Student's Book, which is based on an integrated syllabus that links grammar and communicative functions.

The five documentaries may be used for review or at any point in the course. These sequences correspond to the placement of the review units in the Student's Book, with a fifth "bonus" documentary appearing after Sequence 2. The documentaries are based on authentic, unscripted interviews with people in various situations, and serve to illustrate how language is used by real people in real situations.

Video Activity Book

The Video Activity Book contains sixteen units based on live-action sequences and five documentary units that correspond to the video sequences and documentaries, and is designed to facilitate the effective use of the Video in the classroom. Each unit includes previewing, viewing, and postviewing activities that provide learners with step-by-step support and guidance in understanding and working with the events and language of the sequence. Learners expand their cultural awareness, develop skills and strategies for communicating effectively, and use language creatively.

Video Teacher's Guide

The Video Teacher's Guide contains detailed suggestions for how to use the Video and the Video Activity Book in the classroom, and includes an overview of video teaching techniques, unit-by-unit notes, and a range of optional extension activities. The Video Teacher's Guide also includes answers to the activities in the Video Activity Book and photocopiable transcripts of the video sequences.

◼ VIDEO IN THE CLASSROOM

The use of video in the classroom can be an exciting and effective way to teach and learn. As a medium, video both motivates and entertains students. The *New Interchange* Video is a unique resource that does the following:

- ◼ Depicts dynamic, natural contexts for language use.
- ◼ Presents authentic language as well as cultural information about speakers of English through engaging story lines.
- ◼ Enables learners to use visual information to enhance comprehension.
- ◼ Focuses on the important cultural dimension of learning a language by actually showing how speakers of the language live and behave.
- ◼ Allows learners to observe the gestures, facial expressions, and other aspects of body language that accompany speech.

◼ WHAT EACH UNIT OF THE VIDEO ACTIVITY BOOK CONTAINS

Each unit of the Video Activity Book is divided into four sections: *Preview*, *Watch the Video*, *Follow-up*, and *Language Close-up*. In general, these four sections include, but are not limited to, the following types of activities:

Preview

Culture The culture previews introduce the topics of the video sequences and provide important background and cultural information. They can be presented in class as reading and discussion activities, or students can read and complete them as homework.

Vocabulary The vocabulary activities introduce and practice the essential vocabulary of the video sequences through a variety of interesting tasks.

Guess the Story/Guess the Facts The Guess the Story (or in some units Guess the Facts) activities allow students to make predictions about characters and their actions by watching the video sequences without the sound or by looking at photos in the Video Activity Book. These schema-building activities help to improve students' comprehension when they watch the sequences with the sound.

Watch the Video

Get the Picture These initial viewing activities help students gain global understanding of the sequences by focusing on gist. Activity types vary from unit to unit, but typically involve watching for key information needed to complete a chart, answer questions, or put events in order.

Watch for Details In these activities, students focus on more detailed meaning by watching and listening for specific information to complete tasks about the story line and the characters.

What's Your Opinion? In these activities, students respond to the sequences by making inferences about the characters' actions, feelings, and motivations, and by stating their opinions about issues and topics.

Follow-up

Role Play, Interview, and Other Expansion Activities This section includes communicative activities based on the sequences in which students extend and personalize what they have learned.

Language Close-up

What Did They Say? These cloze activities focus on the specific language in the sequences by having students watch and listen in order to fill in missing words in conversations.

Grammar and Functional Activities In these activities, which are titled to reflect the structural and functional focus of a particular unit, students practice, in a meaningful way, the grammatical structures and functions presented in the video sequences.

First day at class

1 CULTURE

In the United States and Canada, most people have three names:

First name   **Middle name**   **Last name**
Anne   Louise   Lucas

In universities, students usually use titles and last names with their teachers:
Hello, Professor Lucas.

How many names do people have in your country?
Do you use titles (Ms., Mrs., Mr., Professor) with last names?
  With first names?
Do you ever call teachers by their first names?

Hello, Professor Anne.

*In English, do not use a title
with a first name.*

2 VOCABULARY   Nationalities

Pair work   When people first meet, they often talk about nationality.
What do you call people from these countries?

Country	Nationality	Country	Nationality	Country	Nationality
Brazil	Brazilian	France	french	Mexico	Mexican
Canada	Canadian	Japan	Japanese	Spain	Spanish
England	English	Korea	Korean	Thailand	thai

3 GUESS THE STORY

Watch the first minute of the video with the sound off.
What do you think happens to the young man?
Check (✓) your answer.

☐ He meets an old friend.
☑ He meets the teacher of his class.
☐ He goes to the wrong classroom.

 **Watch the video**

4 GET THE PICTURE

Complete the chart. Then compare with a partner.

First name: Sachiko:

Last name: Tanaka

Occupation: Student

First name: Marie

Last name: Ouellette

Occupation: teacher

First name: Rickda

Last name: ?

Occupation: student

5 WATCH FOR DETAILS

Check (✓) the correct answers. Then compare with a partner.

1) Rick is originally from
   - ✓ Mexico.
   - ☐ the United States.
   - ☐ Canada.

2) Rick now lives in
   - ☐ Mexico.
   - ✓ the United States.
   - ☐ Canada.

3) Marie is originally from
   - ☐ France.
   - ✓ Canada.
   - ☐ the United States.

4) Marie teaches
   - ☐ French.
   - ✓ business management.
   - ☐ English.

5) Rick and Sachiko are studying
   - ☐ mathematics.
   - ☐ English.
   - ✓ business management.

6 FORMS OF ADDRESS

How do the people in the video address each other? Check (✓) the
correct answers. Then compare with a partner. (One item has two
answers.)

	First name only	First and last name	Title and last name
1) Marie to Sachiko	☐	☐	✓
2) Marie to Rick	✓	☐	☐
3) Rick to Marie	✓	☐	☐
4) Sachiko to Marie	☐	☐	✓

7 *WHAT'S YOUR OPINION?*

Check (✓) your opinions. Then compare with a partner.

1) Why do you think Rick introduces himself to Marie?
   - ☐ to make a friend
   - ☐ to meet his teacher
   - ☑ other ....

2) When Rick learns that Marie is his teacher, how do you think he feels?
   - ☐ amused
   - ☐ angry
   - ☑ embarrassed
   - ☐ pleased

3) How do you think Marie feels?
   - ☑ amused
   - ☐ angry
   - ☐ embarrassed
   - ☐ pleased

amused

angry

embarrassed

pleased

 *Follow-up*

8 *ROLE PLAY* *Meeting people*

A *Group work* Imagine you are Rick, Sachiko, or Professor Ouellette. Write three more questions to ask each other.

1) *Where are you from?* ....
2) ....
3) ....
4) ....

B Now introduce yourselves. Have conversations like this:

A: Hello, my name's Rick.
B: Hi, I'm Sachiko.
A: Where are you from, Sachiko?
B: I'm from Japan. . . .

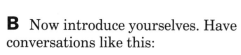

Where are you from?

I'm from Japan.

4

Language close-up

9 *WHAT DID THEY SAY?*

Watch the video and complete the conversation. Then practice it.

Rick is introducing himself to Marie Ouellette.

Rick: Hi. _My_ name's Ricardo, but everybody calls me _Rick_ .

Marie: Well, nice to _mee_ you, Rick. _I'm_ Marie Ouellette.

Rick: It's nice to meet you, Marie. . . . Um, _Where_ are you from, Marie?

Marie: I'm from _Canada_ .

Rick: Oh, so _Canadian_ Canadian?

Marie: That's right.

Rick: From what _city_ ?

Marie: Montreal. How _about_ you?

Rick: I'm originally _from_ Mexico City, but my family and I _live_ up here _now_ .

Marie: Oh, are you a _student_ here?

Rick: Yes, I _am_ .

10 *QUESTIONS WITH* BE

A Complete these questions with **is** or **are**.

1) _Is_ Ms. Tanaka's first name Naomi?
2) _Are_ Rick and Sachiko students?
3) _Are_ you Canadian, Marie?
4) _Is_ Rick from Argentina?
5) _Are_ you a student here, Rick?

B *Pair work* Take turns asking and answering the questions.

A: Is Ms. Tanaka's first name Naomi?
B: No, it isn't. It's . . .

Yes they are
Yes she is
No he is not
Yes he is

11 *WH-QUESTIONS* *Getting to know people*

A Complete these questions with **is**, **are**, or **do**.

1) What _is_ Sachiko's last name?
2) Where _are_ Rick and Sachiko from?
3) What _do_ you teach, Professor Ouellette?
4) What _is_ Rick studying?
5) What _do_ you do, Rick?

B *Pair work* Take turns asking and answering the questions above.

C *Class activity* Now find out about your classmates. Write four more questions. Then go around the class and ask them.

1) _What's your name?_
2) _where are you from?_
3) _She teaches bussine Manag._
4) ....
5) ....

2 I need a change!

Preview

1 CULTURE

THE WORK FORCE IN THE
UNITED STATES AND CANADA

In the United States and Canada, people usually work from
9 A.M. to 5 P.M. Most people get two weeks of vacation a year.
Sometimes people in offices and businesses work late without
extra pay. People also change jobs quite often. The average
person will change careers – not just jobs – two or three times
in a lifetime.

What hours do people work in your country?
How much vacation do they get?
Do they change jobs often?

1959
70%
30%

1991
51%
49%

2 VOCABULARY Occupations

Pair work Who works in the places below? Put the words in the
chart. (One word can go in both columns.) Can you add three
more words?

Hotel	Office
bellhop	computer programmer
Chef	office manager
Cashier	Secretary

bellhop

computer programmer

secretary

office manager

cashier

chef

6

3 GUESS THE STORY

Watch the first minute of the video with the sound off.
Answer these questions.

1) Where do you think the woman works?

2) What do you think her job is?

3) Do you think she likes her work?

 **Watch the video**

4 GET THE PICTURE

Check (✓) the correct answer. Then compare with a partner.

1) What does Lynn do?
   - ☐ She's a hotel worker.
   - ☑ She's a manager.
   - ☐ She's a salesperson.

2) Why doesn't Lynn like her job?
   - ☐ The money isn't good.
   - ☐ She doesn't like her boss.
   - ☑ She works long hours.

3) What does Lynn want to do?
   - ☑ Work in a hotel.
   - ☐ Work for an airline.
   - ☐ Work in a restaurant.

5 WATCH FOR DETAILS

Check (✓) **True** or **False**. Then correct the false statements.
Compare with a partner.

	True	False	
1) Lynn works at CompuTech.	☐	✓	*Lynn works at AdTech.*
2) The company is a computer software company.	☑	☐	
3) Lynn is a manager in customer service.	☑	☐	
4) Lynn works five days a week.	☐	☑	
5) Lynn is studying business.	☐	☑	
6) Bob's friend works in California.	☐	☑	
7) Bob's friend manages a hotel.	☑	☐	

6 GIVING REASONS

Pair work Complete the chart. Look at the pictures and put two possible reasons in each column. (Some reasons can go in both columns.)

Reasons why Lynn doesn't like AdTech	Reasons why Lynn wants to work in a hotel
She works on weekends.	She's interested in hotel management.
There's too much telephon and computer work.	She likes to travel
The company is in a cold climate	She wants to do somethin

She's interested in
hotel management.

She works on
weekends.

She wants to do
something new.

There's too much
telephone and
computer work.

She likes to travel.

The company is
in a cold climate.

Follow-up

7 ROLE PLAY *Jobs*

A *Pair work* Imagine you work at AdTech. Talk about your job:

A: Where do you work at AdTech?
B: . . .
A: What do you do in your job?
B: . . .
A: How do you like your job?
B: . . .

B *Group work* Work in groups of four. Choose a job and ask and answer questions about your work. Who has the most interesting job?

Language close-up

8 WHAT DID THEY SAY?

Watch the video and complete the conversation. Then practice it.

Paula sees Lynn in the cafeteria at lunch.

Paula: Hi, Lynn! How are ...*you*... doing?

Lynn: Oh, *Hi* , Paula. Pretty ...*good* , thanks.
How are you?

Paula: Not ...*bad* . Say, you ...*know* Bob Wallace, don't you?

Lynn: Oh, no, I don't ...*think*... so. Hi, *I'm* Lynn Parker.

Bob: Pleased to ...*meet* you.

Paula: So, ...*How's* everything?

Lynn: *do* you really ...*want* to know?

Paula: Of course *I* do.

9 WH-QUESTIONS WITH DO; *PREPOSITIONS*

A Complete the questions in the present tense. Complete the answers
with the prepositions **at**, **in**, or **to**. Then practice the conversations.

1) Bob: Where ......*do you work*...... , Lynn?

Lynn: I work ...*at*.. AdTech. It's a computer software company.

Bob: What ...*do you do*... there?

Lynn: I'm a manager ...*in*... customer service.

2) Bob: Where ...*do you go*... to school, Lynn?

Lynn: I go ...*to*... Franklin University. I'm studying
hotel management.

> Where do
> you work?

3) Lynn: What ...*do you do*... , Bob?

Bob: I'm a lawyer.

Lynn: Oh. Where ...*do you work*?

Bob: I work ...*at*... the law firm of Christopher Brown.

> I work at
> AdTech.

B *Pair work* Now have similar conversations using your
own information. (If you don't work, choose a job from page 6.)

10 ASKING ABOUT JOBS

Pair work Bob's friend manages a hotel in Hawaii. Think of three
more questions Lynn can ask him about his job. Then ask and
answer the questions.

1) *How do you like your job?* ....

2) ....

3) ....

4) ....

9

Jobs

Preview

1 VOCABULARY Jobs

Pair work Match the jobs and the pictures.

architect   chef   ✓lawyer   photographer   travel agent
cashier   doctor   pianist   teller

1) *lawyer*

2) *architect*

3) *pianist*

4) *cashier*

5) *teller*

6) *doctor*

7) *chef*

8) *photographer*

9) *travel agent*

2 GUESS THE FACTS

Pair work In this documentary, you are going to meet people with the jobs above. Which jobs do you think men do? Which do you think women do?

 *new interchange video* *Watch the video*

3 GET THE PICTURE

What do these people do? Write their occupations under the photos.
Then compare with a partner.

1) *reporter*   2) architect   3) lawyer   4) pianist

5) Computer engineer   6) Cashier   7) teller   8) doctor

4 WATCH FOR DETAILS

Complete the chart. Then compare with a partner.

Rick Armstrong

1) His job: photographer
2) One thing he likes: It's exciting
3) One thing that's difficult: Hard because make fifty o sixty pictures

Sylvia Davis

1) Her job: travel agent travel agent
2) One thing she likes: interisting
3) One thing that's difficult: Sometime is very busy

 *Follow-up*

5 ROLE PLAY   Interview

Class activity   Play the role of a reporter and
interview at least three classmates about their
jobs. Have conversations like the one to the right:

A: What do you do?
B: I'm an architect.
A: Do you like your job? . . .

3 At a garage sale

1 CULTURE

In the United States and Canada, people often sell old things, like furniture, jewelry, or clothing, at a "garage" or "yard" sale. They decide on prices, put the things on tables in their garage or yard, and then put a sign in front of their house. People come to look and maybe to buy. Sometimes the old things are antiques and worth a lot of money.

Do people have garage sales in your country?
What old things do you have at home?
What is one thing that you want to sell?

GARAGE SALE
Saturday, 9 A.M. to 5 P.M. Children's clothes, kitchen items, TV.
257 Maple Avenue

YARD SALE
Sunday, 12 P.M. to 6 P.M. Antiques, books, clock, stereo, bicycle. 89 Shadow Oak Drive

2 VOCABULARY Garage sale items

Pair work Put the words in the chart. Can you add six more words? Add things from your home.

Kitchen items	Jewelry	Other
		books

books

a bracelet

a watch

a necklace

a motorcycle

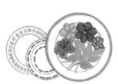
dishes

cups and saucers

a camera

3 GUESS THE STORY

A *Watch the video with the sound off.* Which things do you see at the garage sale? Circle them in Exercise 2.

B What do you think the man buys? What does the woman buy? Make a list.

....

....

....

....

....

....

....

....

---

new interchange video   *Watch the video*

4 WHAT'S YOUR OPINION?

In the end, do you think Fred and Susan buy any of these things at the garage sale? Check (✓) **Yes** or **No**. Then compare with a partner.

	Yes	No
1) the camera	☐	☐
2) the motorcycle	☐	☐
3) the necklace	☐	☐
4) the bracelet	☐	☐
5) the watch	☐	☐

5 MAKING INFERENCES

Check (✓) the best answers. Then complete item (4) with your opinion. Compare with a partner.

1) Susan thinks the camera is
   ☐ too old.
   ☐ too expensive.

2) Fred thinks the necklace is
   ☐ beautiful.
   ☐ just all right.

3) Fred thinks the watch is
   ☐ beautiful.
   ☐ too expensive.

4) The man tells his wife that ....

....

....

13

Follow-up

6 GARAGE SALE

A *Pair work* Imagine you are at a garage sale. Number the sentences below (1 to 6) to make conversations. Then practice the conversations.

1) .... And how much are these earrings?
   ...1... Hello. Can I help you?
   .... It's twelve dollars.
   .... Yes, how much is this bracelet?
   .... They're twenty dollars.
   .... Thanks. I'll think about it.

2) .... Can I help you?
   .... Oh, that's pretty expensive.
   .... OK. I'll take it.
   .... Yes, how much is this watch?
   .... Well, how about thirty dollars?
   .... It's forty dollars.

B *Class activity* Plan a class garage sale. Form two groups. Make a list of things your group will sell, and give each item a price.

Items for sale	Price

Now have the garage sale:

Group A: You are the sellers. Try to sell everything on your list to Group B. Then change roles and decide what to buy from Group B.

Group B: You are the buyers. Ask questions and decide what to buy. Then change roles and try to sell everything on your list to Group A.

Language close-up

7 WHAT DID THEY SAY?

Watch the video and complete the conversation. Then practice it.

Fred and Susan are looking at things at the garage sale.

Fred: Hey, Susan, how do you ......*like*...... this?

Susan: Oh, ... , Fred.

Fred: Oh, come on. It's only a .... !

Susan: .... you really .... it, Fred?

Fred: No, I guess .... right.

Vendor: Can I .... you?

Fred: No, thanks .... We're just ....

Susan: Oh, Fred, ... over here. Just look at this lovely,
          old .... !

Fred: Yeah, it's ....

Susan: It's .... just OK, Fred. It's very .... !

8 EXPRESSING OPINIONS

Fred says these sentences. What do they mean in the video?
Check (✓) the correct answer. Then compare with a partner.

1) How do you like this?
   ☐ Can you believe this?
   ☐ What do you think of this?

2) Oh, come on.
   ☐ Please let me [buy it].
   ☐ Are you kidding?

3) Yeah, it's OK.
   ☐ I like it a little.
   ☐ The price is reasonable.

4) Oh, that's not bad.
   ☐ It's nice.
   ☐ The price is reasonable.

5) Susan, are you kidding?
   ☐ I don't believe it!
   ☐ Let's go!

9 HOW MUCH AND HOW OLD

A Complete the conversations with **how much is (are)** or **how old is (are)**.

1) A: *How much is* .... this necklace?
   B: It's only $10.
   A: .... it?
   B: It's twenty years old.

2) A: .... these books?
   B: They're $2 each.
   A: And .... they?
   B: They're about ten years old.

3) A: .... these shoes?
   B: About two years old, I think.
   A: .... they?
   B: They're $20.

B *Pair work* Practice the conversations. Use items of your own.

4 What kind of movies do you like?

Preview

1 CULTURE

Today, there is a video store in almost every neighborhood in the United States and Canada. Nowadays, many people don't go to the movies very often. Instead they prefer to rent a video and watch it at home. Video stores are large, with every type of video for rent. You can also rent videos in some supermarkets.

Number of stores renting videos (U.S. and Canada)

VIDEO 1993 82,500

VIDEO 1983 13,000

Average Price of

A MOVIE TICKET $5.00   A VIDEO RENTAL $2.50

Do people go to the movies a lot in your country?
Do they rent videos?
What is your favorite movie or video?

2 VOCABULARY Kinds of movies

What kind of movies or videos do you like? Check (✓) your opinions. Then compare answers in groups.

WHAT'S YOUR OPINION?				
	I like them.	They're OK.	I don't like them very much.	I can't stand them.
adventure movies	☐	☐	☐	☐
classic films	☐	☐	☐	☐
comedies	☐	☐	☐	☐
horror films	☐	☐	☐	☐
science-fiction movies	☐	☐	☐	☐
suspense movies	☐	☐	☐	☐

Indiana Jones and the Last Crusade

Dracula

Eyes of Laura Mars

Star Trek III

Heaven Help Us

3 GUESS THE STORY

Watch the first two minutes of the video with the sound off.
Answer these questions.

1) Are the young men friends?   2) What are they doing?   3) What's the problem?

 **Watch the video**

4 GET THE PICTURE

Check (✓) **True** or **False**. Then compare with a partner.

	True	False
1) Pat, Alfredo, and Bill all like movies.	☐	☐
2) Nobody likes science fiction.	☐	☐
3) They can't agree on a movie.	☐	☐
4) They decide to go to a country and western concert.	☐	☐

Pat   Alfredo   Bill

5 MAKING INFERENCES

What do Pat, Bill, and Alfredo like? Write **Y** (yes), or **N** (no). Then compare in groups. (Sometimes they don't say exactly, but try to give your opinion.)

	Pat	Bill	Alfredo
Movies			
science fiction	Y	N	
suspense thrillers		Y	
classic films			
horror films			
westerns			
Music			
country and western			
jazz			

6 WHAT'S THE PROBLEM?

Pair work Answer these questions.

1) Which person is difficult to please?
2) Do you know anyone like this?

Alfredo   Bill   Pat

 *Follow-up*

7 FINISH THE STORY

Group work What do you think happens in the end?
Finish the story.

8 MAKING PLANS

Group work Plan what to do this evening. Choose
one of these activities. Give your opinions like this:

There's a great .... tonight at ....
Do you really like .... ?
That sounds good. How about you, ... ?
I don't really like ....
Well, what kind of .... do you like?

THE Country Gold Club

presents   *country and western music*   THE BLUE RIDGE TRIO

Showtimes:
8:30 p.m. and 11 p.m.
236 North Hill Street
555-8123

The ★ Star Movie Theater

SCIENCE FICTION
Alien Abduction
White Mountains, Arizona

VISITORS FROM SPACE

8:00 p.m. 10:00 p.m.

The Back Door
NEW ORLEANS JAZZ BAND

Shows: 9 p.m. and 11 p.m.
Credit Cards Reservations
(555-6073)

"The BEST comedy of the year!"

"The funniest movie
I've seen all year!"
—B. Jones

"Wildly funny!"
The Times

Home Again

The Main Street Theater
7:30 PM   9:30 PM

Language close-up

9 WHAT DID THEY SAY?

Watch the video and complete the conversation. Then practice it.

Bill, Alfredo, and Pat are trying to decide how to spend the evening.

Bill: So, . . . what ..*do*.. we ..*do*.. now?

Alfredo: What .... is it?

Bill: .... o'clock.

Pat: Look, ... all like .... Why don't we
           .... a video and .... it at my .... ?

Bill: That's .... a bad .... , Pat.

Alfredo: It's .... with ....

Pat: Well, then, ... on! . . . Now here .... some
           great ....-fiction movies! .... do
           you .... , Bill?

Bill: Uh, I can't .... sci-fi. How .... a good
           .... thriller?

Pat: Uh . . . Alfredo, ... about you? .... do you
           .... of science .... ?

Alfredo: Oh, it's ....

Alfredo   Bill   Pat

10 OBJECT PRONOUNS

A Fill in the blanks with **him**, **her**, **it**, or **them**.

1) A: Do you like horror films?
   B: No, I can't stand ...*them*... .

2) A: Who's your favorite actress?
   B: Michelle Pfeiffer. I like .... a lot.

3) A: Do you like rap music?
   B: Yes, I like .... a lot.

4) A: What do you think of Robert DeNiro?
   B: I don't like .... at all.

5) A: Do you like westerns?
   B: No, I don't like .... very much.

6) A: What do you think of science fiction?
   B: I like .... a lot.

B *Pair work* Take turns asking and answering the questions above.
Give your own opinions.

11 EXPRESSING LIKES AND DISLIKES

Pair work Take turns giving opinions about movies, actors, and actresses.
Your partner responds with surprise, as in the conversations below.

1) A: I can't stand science fiction!
   B: Really?

2) A: I love Julia Roberts.
   B: Are you kidding?

3) A: I hate old movies.
   B: Is that right?

4) A: I think Tom Cruise is fantastic.
   B: Do you really like Tom Cruise?

Documentary 2
What's your favorite kind of music?

Preview

1 VOCABULARY Kinds of music

Class activity In this documentary, some people are going to talk about music. How many kinds of music can you think of? List them.

Watch the video

2 GET THE PICTURE

How many different kinds of music do people talk about? Check (✓) them. Then compare with a partner.

- ☐ classical
- ☑ country and western
- ☐ folk
- ☐ jazz
- ☐ new wave
- ☐ pop
- ☐ rap
- ☐ rhythm and blues (R & B)
- ☐ rock

3 WATCH FOR DETAILS

A What kind(s) of music do these people like? Check (✓) all correct answers. Then compare with a partner.

	1	2	3	4	5	6
country and western	✓	☐	☐	☐	☐	☐
jazz	☐	☐	☐	☐	☐	☐
rock	☐	☐	☐	☐	☐	☐
classical	☐	☐	☐	☐	☐	☐
new wave	☐	☐	☐	☐	☐	☐

B Which people play a musical instrument? Write **S** for saxophone,
G for guitar, or **P** for piano. Then compare with a partner. (One person
doesn't play an instrument.)

saxophone

guitar

piano

1) ....   2) ....   3) ....   4) ....   5) ....

4 THE REPORTER'S QUESTIONS

What interview questions does the reporter ask? Check (✓) them.
Then compare with a partner.

✓ How often do you get to go to nightclubs?	☐ Do you play a musical instrument (yourself)?
☐ What's your favorite kind of music?	☐ What do you think of country and western music?
☐ Do you like rap?	
☐ How often do you listen to live music?	☐ Where's a good place to go dancing?
☐ What's your least favorite kind of music?	☐ How often do you go dancing?
☐ Do you like classical music?	☐ What's your favorite nightclub?

Follow-up

5 CLASS INTERVIEW

A *Class activity* Use the questions in Exercise 4
to interview at least three classmates. Have
conversations like this:

A: How often do you go to nightclubs?
B: About twice a week.
A: What's your favorite kind of music?
B: Country.

B Now tell about the people you interviewed. What kinds of
music are the most popular? Least popular?

5 A family picnic

1 CULTURE

In the United States and Canada, 97 percent of all people say that family is the most important part of life. But people in the U.S. and Canada move often, and children often leave home at age 18. Many families only see each other on important holidays or at family parties.

- Six percent of all families move every year.
- On an average day, 116,438 people move.
- People often live far away from their parents and grandparents.
- Only 36 percent of families see their relatives once a week.

In the U.S. and Canada, 70 percent of all husbands and wives say they're happy with each other.

In your country, when do children leave home?
Do children live near their parents and grandparents?
When do families see each other?

2 VOCABULARY Family

Pair work How are these people related to Jane? Fill in the blanks in her family tree.

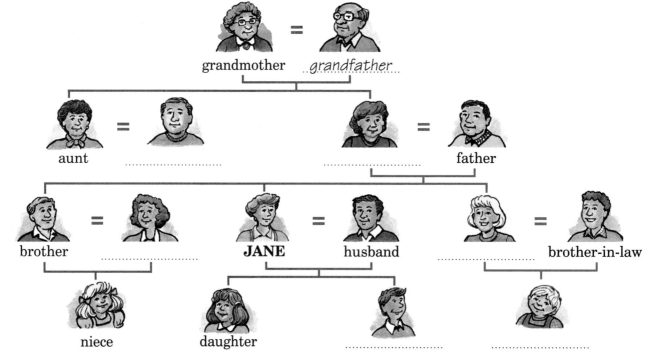

22

3 GUESS THE STORY

Watch the first minute of the video with the sound off.
The young man takes his friend Betsy to a family picnic.
Who do you think she meets? Look at the photo and list
five more people.

1) _his mother_   4) ....

2) ....   5) ....

3) ....   6) ....

 **Watch the video**

4 GET THE PICTURE

Who's at the picnic? Check (✓) **Yes** or **No**. Then compare with
a partner.

	Yes	No
1) Rick's parents	✓	☐
2) his brother	☐	☐
3) his brother's wife	☐	☐
4) his niece	☐	☐
5) his grandparents	☐	☐
6) his younger sister	☐	☐
7) his older sister	☐	☐
8) his aunt	☐	☐

5 WATCH FOR DETAILS

Check (✓) the correct answer. Then compare with a partner.

1) Rick's grandmother lives in
   ✓ Mexico.
   ☐ New Mexico.

2) Rick has
   ☐ one brother and a sister.
   ☐ one brother and two sisters.

3) Rick's brother Freddy
   ☐ is a doctor.
   ☐ owns a business.

4) Freddy's wife Linda manages
   ☐ a boutique.
   ☐ a bookstore.

5) Angela is
   ☐ three years old.
   ☐ four years old.

6) Rick knows Betsy from
   ☐ work.
   ☐ night school.

6 WHAT'S YOUR OPINION?

Pair work Read the culture box on page 22 again. Is Rick's family like most families in the United States and Canada? How is it the same and how is it different?

 *Follow-up*

7 YOUR FAMILY

A *Pair work* Is your family like Rick's? Tell about your family and find out about your partner's. Ask questions like these:

Are you living with your parents right now?
Are you married?
Do you have any children?
How old are they?
Do you have any brothers and sisters?
Are they still going to school or are they working?

B Draw a simple picture (or show your partner a photo) of your family. Your partner will ask questions about each person.

Is this your sister?
What does she do?
Is she studying English?

8 AN INTERESTING PERSON

A *Pair work* Find out about your partner's most interesting relative or friend. Ask questions like these:

Who's your most interesting relative or friend?
What's his/her name?
What does he/she do?
Where is he/she living at the moment?
How old is he/she?
Is he/she married?

B Now tell another classmate about the person like this:

Yong Su has an interesting cousin.
Her name is Son Hee.
She owns a travel agency.
She's from Seoul.
She's working in New York at the moment.
She's 30 years old.

Language close-up

9 WHAT DID THEY SAY?

Watch the video and complete the conversation. Then practice it.

Betsy and Rick are arriving at the picnic.

Betsy: So, how many ....*people*........ are there in your ....*family*........ , Rick?

Rick: A .... , if you count all my ....

Betsy: Do they all .... here in the .... now?

Rick: Oh, ... I have relatives in .... My grandmother and .... are there, and my older .... , too.

Betsy: How many .... do you have?

Rick: .... , plus an older .... There's my .... Freddy over there with his .... Linda.

Betsy: Oh, really. What do they .... ?

Rick: Freddy .... an import-export business, and Linda manages .... boutique.

Betsy: Is that their .... ?

Rick: Yeah. Her ....'s Angela.

---

10 PRESENT CONTINUOUS VS. SIMPLE PRESENT
Asking about relatives

A Complete the conversation using the present continuous or simple present. Then practice with a partner.

A: Do all of your relatives live in the United States?

B: No, I ....*have*........ (have) relatives in Mexico. My grandparents and older sister .... (live) there.

A: What does your sister do? Does she have a job?

B: No, she .... (work) right now. She .... (go) to school.

A: Really? What is she studying?

B: She .... (study) English literature. She .... (love) it.

A: What about your grandparents? Are they still working or are they retired?

B: They .... (work)! And they're both 80 years old!

B *Class activity* Now write similar questions of your own. Then go around the class and interview your classmates about their families.

1) *Do your parents live in . . . ?* ....

2) ....

3) ....

4) ....

6 I like to stay in shape.

1 CULTURE

In the United States and Canada, most people nowadays think regular exercise is important. They exercise at home, or at a gym or health club. They play sports after school, after work, and on weekends. They also bicycle, walk, swim, or jog. People exercise for different reasons: to lose weight, to stay in shape, or just to relax.

Do you exercise or play sports?
What sports are popular in your country?

In the U.S. and Canada:

 Thirty-five percent of people exercise every day.

 Eighteen percent of people play team sports regularly.

2 VOCABULARY Sports and exercise

A ***Pair work*** Here are some things people do to stay in shape. Write the words under the pictures.

aerobics   basketball   ✓jogging   soccer   swimming   volleyball

1) *jogging* ....

2) ....

3) ....

4) ....

5) ....

6) ....

B Put the words in the chart. Can you add two more words?

Individual activities		Team sports	
jogging	....	....	....
....	....	....	....

26

I like to stay in shape.

3 GUESS THE STORY

Watch the first minute of the video with the sound off.
Who do you think likes to exercise more, the woman or the man?

Watch the video

4 GET THE PICTURE

Check (✓) **True** or **False**. Correct the false statements. Then compare
with a partner.

	True	*False*	
1) Mark is a friend of Anne's.	☐	☐	....
2) Mark really likes to exercise.	☐	☐	....
3) Anne is in better shape than Mark.	☐	☐	....

5 WATCH FOR DETAILS

A How does Mark stay in shape? Check (✓)
the things he *says* he does.

B Which things do you think he *really* does?
Circle them. Then compare with a partner.

☐ He jogs to stay in shape.

☐ He gets up early.

☐ He bicycles.

☐ He does aerobics.

☐ He swims.

☐ He goes to the health club.

☐ He takes long walks.

☐ He plays tennis.

☐ He plays team sports.

6 WHAT'S YOUR OPINION?

Pair work What kind of person is Anne? What kind of person is Mark? Choose at least one word for each person.

Anne	Mark
....	....
....	....
....	....

friendly

intelligent

polite

pushy

Follow-up

7 INTERVIEW

A Pair work Add three questions to the list about sports and exercise.

1) What kinds of sports do you play?
2) What kinds of exercise do you do?
3) Are you in good shape?

4) ....
5) ....
6) ....

B Take turns asking and answering your questions. Your partner will answer playing the role of Anne or Mark.

8 HOW ABOUT YOU?

A Complete the chart. Then compare with a partner.

Things you sometimes do	Things you don't usually do
I sometimes . . . . after school.	I don't usually . . . . on the weekend.
....	....
....	....
Things you never do	
I never go . . . . in the morning.	
....	
....	

B Class activity Who in the class likes to exercise? Who doesn't? Make a class chart.

Language close-up

9 WHAT DID THEY SAY?

Watch the video and complete the conversation.
Then practice it.

Anne is jogging in the park when Mark introduces himself.

Mark: Hi there. Nice ....day...., isn't it?

Anne: Oh, yes, very ....

Mark: Do you .... come out here this .... ?

Anne: Usually. I like to stay in ....

Mark: I do, too. I .... get up around .... o'clock.

Anne: Oh, ... ?

Mark: Yeah. I .... start with some .... There's a .... aerobics program on TV at ....

Anne: No .... ! I guess you really do .... to stay in shape.

Mark: Hey, ... days a .... I go straight to my health club after ....

10 ADVERBS OF FREQUENCY

A Put the adverbs in the correct place. Write the sentences.

1) I get up before 5 A.M. (never)
   I never get up before 5 A.M. ....

2) I don't have a big breakfast. (usually)
   ....

3) I play tennis after work. (sometimes)
   ....

4) I take a long walk on the weekend. (often)
   ....

5) I watch TV. (never)
   ....

6) I jog in the morning. (always)
   ....

B Imagine you are Mark. Change the frequency adverbs in the sentences where necessary. Compare with a partner.

C How often do you do these things? Use the phrases below or ones of your own. Then compare with a partner.

| every evening | very often | about three times a month |
| twice a week | once a year | every day |

1) go to sleep by 10 P.M.
   ....

2) work late
   ....

3) ride a bicycle
   ....

4) do aerobics
   ....

29

How was your trip to San Francisco?

1 CULTURE

More than two million people visit San Francisco every year. San Francisco is famous for its shops, its restaurants, its beautiful old buildings, and its cable cars. San Francisco's Chinatown is an important part of the city. There are more than 80,000 people living in Chinatown. San Francisco is also famous for fog and hills. In fact, the city is built on 43 hills!

There are more than 3,300 restaurants in San Francisco!

Do you know anything else about San Francisco?
Would you like to visit San Francisco?
What cities in North America would you like to visit?

2 VOCABULARY Places in San Francisco

Pair work How much do you know about San Francisco?
Write the names under the pictures.

Fisherman's Wharf   Chinatown   The Japanese Tea Garden
The Golden Gate Bridge   ✓A cable car   Ghirardelli Square

1) *A cable car*

2) ....

3) ....

4) ....

5) ....

6) ....

3 GUESS THE STORY

Watch the video with the sound off. Which of the things in Exercise 2 do you think the woman and her husband see? Write a check (✓) next to them.

 Watch the video

4 GET THE PICTURE

A Look at your answers to Exercise 3. Did you guess correctly?

B Correct the mistakes in Phyllis's travel diary. Then compare with a partner.

DAY	NOTES
FRIDAY <s>sight-seeing</s> work	*Fisherman's Wharf was my favorite place!*
SATURDAY work	
SUNDAY *morning: sight-seeing*	

5 WATCH FOR DETAILS

What did Phyllis and her husband do in these places? Check (✓) the correct answers. Then compare with a partner.

1) Ghirardelli Square
   - ☐ They bought some clothes.
   - ☐ They bought some postcards.

2) Fisherman's Wharf
   - ☐ They bought some souvenirs.
   - ☐ They had lunch.

3) Golden Gate Park
   - ☐ They visited a tea garden.
   - ☐ They had lunch.

4) Chinatown
   - ☐ They walked for hours.
   - ☐ They visited a temple.

Follow-up

6 A DAY IN SAN FRANCISCO

A *Group work* Which things to see in San Francisco seem most
interesting to you? Number them from 1 to 6 (1 = the most interesting).

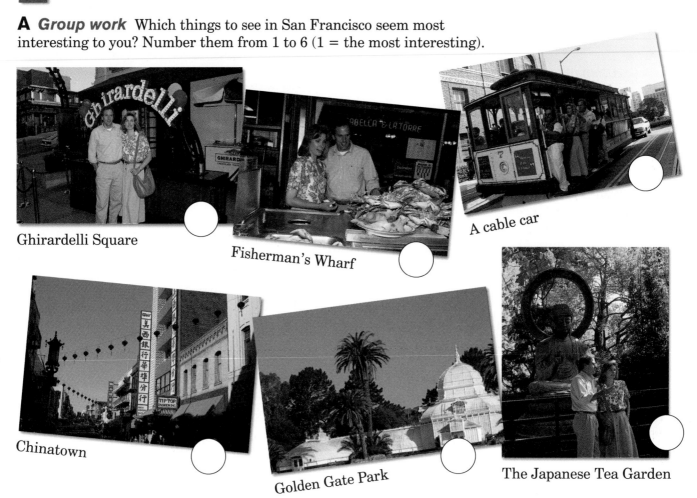

Ghirardelli Square

Fisherman's Wharf

A cable car

Chinatown

Golden Gate Park

The Japanese Tea Garden

B Plan an afternoon in San Francisco. Choose three places to visit
or things to do.

7 WHAT'S YOUR OPINION?

A *Pair work* What do you like to do when you visit a new city?
Number them from 1 to 5. Can you add three things to the list?

.... go sight-seeing   1) ....
.... eat at local restaurants   2) ....
.... buy souvenirs   3) ....
.... take photographs
.... go shopping

B Now compare answers with another pair. Have conversations like this:

A: Do you like to go shopping?
B: No, I don't. I hate to go shopping.

Language close-up

8 WHAT DID THEY SAY?

Watch the video and complete the conversation. Then practice it.

Phyllis and Yoko are on their way to work.

Yoko: Hi, Phyllis.
Phyllis: Hi, Yoko. ...*How*... have you been?
Yoko: Oh, ... How .... you?
Phyllis: Great! Just .... !
Yoko: So, ... was your .... to San Francisco?
Phyllis: Fantastic! We really .... it.
Yoko: Well, that .... surprise me. I love to ....
San Francisco. Uh, so, your .... went with you?
Phyllis: Yes. I .... on Friday, and Bill had business to do in
the .... , too.
Yoko: Oh, that's .... So, what did you do over the .... ?
Phyllis: We went .... together all day Saturday and
Sunday ....
Yoko: Oh, really? .... me about it.

9 PAST TENSE Describing a trip

A Fill in the blanks with the correct past tense forms of the verbs in
parentheses. Then practice the conversations.

1) Yoko: Tell me about your trip to San Francisco.
Phyllis: Well, we ....*did*... (do) a lot of interesting things. Naturally,
we .... (start) Saturday morning with a ride on a cable car.
Yoko: Naturally! And then?
Phyllis: Then we .... (go) straight to Ghirardelli Square to do some shopping.
Yoko: Isn't it wonderful? I .... (go) there the last time I .... (be)
in San Francisco.

2) Yoko: .... you .... (visit) Alcatraz Island?
Phyllis: No, we .... (have / not) time.
Yoko: Oh, what .... you .... (do) then?
Phyllis: We .... (take) a cab to Golden Gate Park.
Yoko: Great! .... you .... (see) the Japanese Tea Garden?
Phyllis: Oh, yes, it .... (be) really beautiful. But, to tell the truth,
the thing we .... (like) best .... (be) Chinatown.

B *Pair work* Have similar conversations about a real or imaginary trip of
your own. Start like this:

A: I went to . . .
B: Really! Tell me about your trip. . . .

8 Are you sure it's all right?

Preview

1 CULTURE

In the United States and Canada, people often invite friends to their homes for a
meal or a party. Here are some simple rules to follow:
- When someone invites you to dinner, do not bring anyone with you. Your host
  will tell you if you can bring a guest, such as your husband or wife.
- When someone invites you to a party, you can often bring a friend. But always
  call your host first to ask if it's OK.

PARTY

Date: June 15
Time: 8:00 P.M.
Place: 26 Elm St.
Apt. 2C
Bring a Friend!

In your country, do people often invite friends to their home for dinner?
Is it OK to bring a friend to dinner? To a party?

2 VOCABULARY Places

Pair work Write the numbers of the places on the map. (There is one extra place.)

1) There's a **coffee shop** on the corner of Hennepin and Lagoon.
2) There's a **movie theater** on Hennepin, just before the coffee shop.
3) There's a **drugstore** across the street from the movie theater.
4) There's a **parking lot** on Lagoon, next door to the coffee shop.
5) Your friend's **apartment building** is across the street from the parking lot.

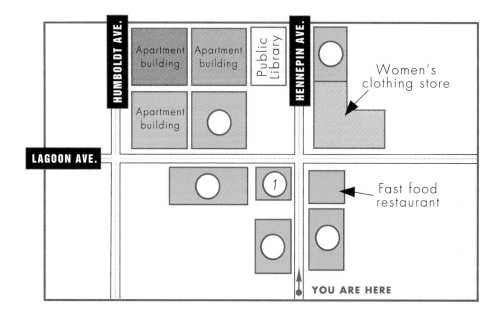

3 GUESS THE STORY

Watch the first minute of the video with the sound off.
These people are going to a party. What do you think
happens? Check (✓) your answer.

☐ They get lost.
☐ They go on the wrong day.
☐ They arrive too late.

 Watch the video

4 GET THE PICTURE

A Check (✓) the correct answers. Then compare with a partner.

	Katy	Bill	Pat	Sandy
1) Who is having a party?	☐	☐	☐	☐
2) Who did (s)he invite?	☐	☐	☐	☐
3) Who didn't (s)he invite?	☐	☐	☐	☐
4) Who is a good friend of Katy's?	☐	☐	☐	☐

B What mistake do Bill, Pat, and Sandy make? Did you guess
correctly in Exercise 3?

5 WATCH FOR DETAILS

Correct the mistakes below. Then compare with a partner.

Pat, Bill, and ~~Katy~~ *Sandy* are going to a party at ~~Sandy's~~ *Katy's* apartment. The

party is very formal. Pat doesn't remember the exact address, but he

remembers there's a coffee shop just before you turn. When they arrive,

they don't hear any music. It's a little late. The party was last week.

35

6 WHAT'S YOUR OPINION?

Pair work Answer these questions.

1) Is it OK for Bill to take
Sandy and Pat to the party?
☐ Yes, it's fine.
☐ No. It's not a good idea.
☐ I'm not sure.

2) How do you think Katy feels
when her friends arrive?
☐ amused
☐ angry
☐ surprised
☐ other ....

3) How do you think Pat and
Sandy feel?
☐ embarrassed
☐ angry
☐ amused
☐ other ....

Follow-up

7 INVITING

Group work Invite two or three classmates to one of these activities.

the beach

the movies

a party

a soccer game

Start like this:

A: *(Name of classmate)* invited me to .... on
Sunday. Do you want to come?
B: Are you sure it's OK?
A: Of course it is! .... is a good friend of mine.
C: Well, I don't know. Why don't you ask .... first? . . .

8 ROLE PLAY *A surprise guest*

A *Group work* Work in groups of four. Play the roles
of Katy, Sandy, Bill, and Pat. Knock on Katy's door and
act out the situation three times.

1) The first time, act out the conversation just like
in the video.
2) The second time, imagine Katy is busy and
doesn't want company.
3) The third time, make up your own ending.

B Now act out your third conversation for the
class. Who has the best ending?

Language close-up

9 WHAT DID THEY SAY?

Watch the video and complete the conversation. Then practice it.

Pat, Bill, and Sandy are going to Katy's party. Pat is asking for directions.

Pat: OK. Well, we're at the ...... *corner* ...... of 31st Street. ...*Now*... what?

Bill: Well, I don't remember her .... ,
        but I know she lives .... here.

Pat: Fine. But do I go .... , right, or straight
        .... ?

Bill: .... ahead. . . . I remember there's
        a .... theater just before you ....

Pat: Hey, is .... it?

Bill: No, I .... think so. . . . There was a coffee
        shop .... door and a drugstore ....
        the street.

Sandy: Oh, I don't see a .... Well, there's a Vietnamese
        .... with a bookstore .... to it.

Pat: Yeah, and no .... shop either. Hey, look! There's another
        movie theater up ahead on the ....

Bill: Great! .... a drugstore.

10 LOCATIONS

A Look at the map of Katy's neighborhood. Answer
the questions using these prepositions.

    across from   near   next to
    on the corner of   on

1) Where's the Suburban World Theater?
   It's across from the Vietnamese restaurant.

2) Where's Border's Book Shop?
   ....

3) Where's Figlio's Restaurant?
   ....

4) Where's the Rainbow Cafe?
   ....

5) Where's the clothing store?
   ....

B *Pair work* Now ask similar questions about
places near your school.

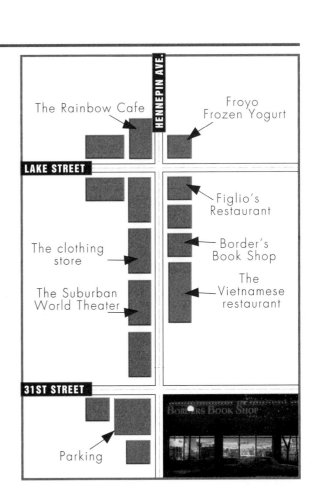

Documentary 3
In a suburban home

Preview

1 VOCABULARY Guess the rooms of a house

Pair work Match the words and the photos.

child's bedroom   family room   ✓kitchen
dining room   guest room   living room

1) *kitchen*

2) ....

3) ....

4) ....

5) ....

6) ....

Watch the video

2 GET THE PICTURE

A Look at your answers to Exercise 1. Were they correct?

B What is one thing the Bartlett family does in each room? Complete the sentences. Then compare with a partner.

1) In the kitchen, they ....
2) In the dining room, they ....
3) In the family room, they ....

38

3 WATCH FOR DETAILS

Write down all of the things you see in each room. Then combine
answers in groups. Which group has the most things on its list?

1) the kitchen	2) the dining room	3) the living room	4) Matthew's room
a sink			
5) the guest room	**6) Daniel's room**	**7) the large bedroom**	**8) the family room**

4 WHAT'S YOUR OPINION?

Pair work Answer these questions.

1) Do you like the Bartletts' home? Name one thing that you
   like. Is there anything you don't like?
2) Is the Bartlett home like homes in your country? How is
   it different?

 *Follow-up*

5 YOUR HOME

Group work Find out about the homes or apartments
your classmates live in. Ask questions like these:

1) Do you live in a city?
2) How big is your home?
3) What are some interesting things in your home?
4) What's your favorite room?

Do you live
in a city?

No, I live
on a farm.

9 Help is coming.

1 CULTURE

To protect their homes against crime, people in the United States and Canada:
- Put special locks on their doors.
- Leave lights on when they go out.
- Have a "peephole" (or hole in the door) to see who's outside.
- Buy an alarm that makes noise if someone opens the door or window.
- Buy a dog.

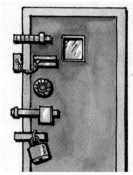

On an average day in the U.S., people spend over $2 million on home security.

What other ways can you protect your home?
How do people protect their homes in your country?

2 VOCABULARY Physical appearance

A *Pair work* Write the words and phrases in the chart. (One of the words can go in two places.) Can you add two more words or phrases?

✓early forties   late forties   short   blond   elderly
long   curly   tall   bald

Age	Height	Hair
early forties		

B List two ways to describe the man and two to describe the woman.

The man	The woman
late forties	

40

3 GUESS THE STORY

Watch the first minute of the video with the sound off.
Who do you think comes to the couple's house?

 Watch the video

4 GET THE PICTURE

What really happens? Check (✓) your answer. Then compare
with a partner.

☐ Strange men come to the door.
☐ Dave's cousin comes to visit.
☐ The prisoners come to the house.
☐ Some friends come to visit.

5 WATCH FOR DETAILS

Put the pictures in order (1 to 6). Then write the correct sentence
under each picture. Compare with a partner.

✓Sarah and Dave are reading.
  Dave is calling the police.
  The men are standing in the driveway.

Sarah is looking at the minivan.
The men are getting out of the minivan.
The men are introducing themselves to Sarah and Dave.

....

....

....

....

....

....

Sarah and Dave are
reading.

....

....

....

....

6 DESCRIBING SOMEONE

A Circle the correct answers. Then compare with a partner.

		George		Don	
1) Age	twenties	(forties)		twenties	forties
2) Hair color	blond	brown		blond	brown
3) Height	tall	short		tall	short
4) Type of shirt	short-sleeved	long-sleeved		short-sleeved	long-sleeved
5) Other	baseball cap	no hat		baseball cap	no hat
	glasses	no glasses		glasses	no glasses

B What else can you add about George and Don? Compare your descriptions. Who has the best description?

Follow-up

7 THE RIGHT DECISION?

Pair work Sarah and Dave call the police. What is the best thing to do in a situation like this?

☐ Call the police.
☐ Open the door and ask, "Who's there?"
☐ Call a friend or relative.
☐ other ....

8 WHAT HAPPENS NEXT?

A *Group work* What do you think happens when the police arrive? Write out the conversation between Sarah, Dave, and the police. Start like this:

Officer: Is there a problem here?
Dave: Well, uh, . . .

B *Class activity* Act out your conversation for the class.

Language close-up

9 WHAT DID THEY SAY?

Watch the video and complete the conversation. Then practice it.

Sarah and Dave are relaxing at home.

Sarah: Would you ....*like*...... another cup of .....*coffee*........ ?
Dave: ...., thanks. I don't .... so.
Sarah: Is there anything .... in the .... ?
Dave: Well, there's something about a .... escape.
Sarah: Oh, really?
Dave: Yeah. A couple of .... escaped from the state
　　　prison in a .... van.
Sarah: Hmm . . . . we know .... with a minivan?
Dave: A minivan? What .... is it?
Sarah: I .... know. Light .... , maybe,
　　　or .... I can't .... very well.
Dave: Where is this .... ?
Sarah: It's parked right in .... of the ....
　　　And there are .... guys in it.

10 MODIFIERS WITH PARTICIPLES AND PREPOSITIONS

A Look at the picture. Match the information in columns A, B, and C.

A	B	C
Sarah	is the young one	holding his hat
Dave	is the heavy one	with glasses
George	is the blonde woman	wearing a green shirt
Don	is the bald man	wearing a blue T-shirt

B *Pair work* What else do you remember about the people in the video? Write at least three more sentences of your own.

1) ....　3) ....

2) ....

11 DESCRIBING SOMEONE

A *Pair work* Take turns asking and answering questions about a classmate. Try to guess who the person is.

A: Is it a tall person with short hair?
B: No, the person is short . . .

B Write five sentences describing your classmates. Two of your sentences should be false. Then read your sentences. Your partner says **True** or **False** and corrects the false sentences.

A: Steve's the tall guy wearing a blue shirt.
B: False. He's wearing a white shirt.

10 Sorry I'm late.

1 CULTURE

In the United States and Canada, people usually like others to be on time,
but for some occasions it's OK to be a little late.

For class or a business appointment,	**plan to arrive**	on time or a little early.
When you meet a friend,		on time or 5 to 10 minutes late.
When someone invites you to dinner,		about 10 to 15 minutes late.
For an informal party,		a little late (15 to 30 minutes).

Are people usually on time for appointments in your country?
Is it OK to arrive late when you meet a friend for dinner? When you
go to an informal party?

2 VOCABULARY *Past tense of verbs*

Pair work Do you know the past tense of these verbs? Complete the chart.

Present	Past	Present	Past
call	*called*	lock	
do		open	
find		pay	
get		remember	
go		send	
leave		start	

3 GUESS THE STORY

Watch the first minute of the video with the sound off.
What do you think happened? Check (✓) all correct answers.

- ☐ The man arrived very late for dinner.
- ☐ The woman was angry.
- ☐ The man didn't have his wallet.
- ☐ The woman paid for dinner.

Watch the video

4 GET THE PICTURE

What really happened? Check (✓) the correct answers. Then compare with a partner.

1) What was the problem with Tom's car?
   - ☐ It didn't start.
   - ☐ He locked his keys in it.
   - ☐ He forgot to buy gasoline.

2) What was the problem with Tom's wallet?
   - ☐ He left it in the car.
   - ☐ He lost it.
   - ☐ He had no money in it.

3) Who paid for dinner?
   - ☐ Tom paid.
   - ☐ Marie paid.
   - ☐ Tom and Marie each paid half.

5 WATCH FOR DETAILS

A Put the pictures in order (1 to 6). Then write the correct sentence under each picture. Compare with a partner.

Tom remembered his wallet was in the house.
Tom tried to call Marie.
Tom called a lock service.

Tom remembered his wallet was in the car.
Tom saw his keys inside the car.
✓Tom left the house and started his car.

Tom left the house and started his car.

B *Pair work* What else happened? Can you add two things?

1) ....

2) ....

6 WHAT'S YOUR OPINION?

Pair work Complete the chart. Check (✓) the words that describe
Tom and Marie.

	Angry	*Upset*	*Tired*	*Embarrassed*	*Understanding*	*Worried*
Tom	☐	☐	☐	☐	☐	☐
Marie	☐	☐	☐	☐	☐	☐

 *Follow-up*

7 QUESTION GAME

A Write three more questions about the story. Use the past tense
and **how**, **why**, **how much**, **who**, or **where**.

1) *Why did Tom go back to his apartment?*
2) *When did Tom lock his keys in the car?*
3) ....
4) ....
5) ....

B *Pair work* Answer your partner's questions. If you don't think
the answer was in the video, say **It didn't say**.

8 TELL THE STORY

Pair work Write out the story using **first**, **after that**, **next**,
then, and **finally**. Include one mistake. Then read your story
to another pair. Can they find the mistake?

First, Tom left his apartment and started . . . .
....
....
....
....
....
....
....

Language close-up

9 WHAT DID THEY SAY?

Watch the video and complete the conversation. Then practice it.

Marie is waiting for Tom in the restaurant when he arrives late.

Marie: Hi. ......*There*...... will be ...*two*... of us. . . . Thank you. . . .

Tom: Marie! I'm really .... How ....
have you been waiting?

Marie: It's .... , Tom. I've only .... here
for a little .... Is everything all .... ?

Tom: Yes, it is .... , but you won't .... what
just happened to ....

Marie: Well, what .... ?

Tom: Well, ... of all, I was a little ....
leaving my .... , and so I was in a
.... Then, just after I .... the car,
I .... I didn't have any ....
with me, so I went .... to get my ....

Marie: Did you .... it?

Tom: Oh, yes! I .... it. That wasn't the ....
The problem .... when I got .... to
my .... , I couldn't .... in.

Marie: Do you mean you .... your keys in the car?

Tom: That's .... So, guess what I did .... that!

Marie: I .... guess.

10 PRESENT PERFECT

A *Pair work* Write questions using **Have you ever . . . ?** and the correct
forms of the verbs in parentheses. Can you add three questions to the list?

1) *Have you ever locked* .... (lock) your keys in the car?

2) .... (call) a lock service?

3) .... (leave) your wallet in the car?

4) .... (arrive) late for an important dinner?

5) .... (go) to a restaurant without money?

6) .... (wait) a long time for someone in a restaurant?

7) ....

8) ....

9) ....

B *Class activity* Go around the class and interview at least three classmates.
Who answered "yes" to the most questions?

Across the Golden Gate Bridge

1 CULTURE

The city of San Francisco is surrounded by water on three sides. To the east, the Oakland Bay Bridge crosses San Francisco Bay to the city of Berkeley, home of the Berkeley campus of the University of California. To the north, visitors can see the famous Golden Gate Bridge. The first stop across this bridge is Sausalito, a beautiful town with shops and restaurants on the water. A short drive away is the redwood forest Muir Woods. It has some of the tallest trees in the world. Less than an hour away by car is the Napa Valley, famous for some of California's best wine.

Do you know any other places near San Francisco?
When you visit a city, do you use the bus or train, or do you rent a car?

2 VOCABULARY *Taking a trip*

Pair work Match the pictures with the words in the glossary below.

1) .winery...........................

2) ....

3) ....

4) ....

5) ....

6) ....

bay a wide opening of water that is an entrance to the sea
forest an area of land covered with trees
valley an area of land between two hills or mountains

vineyard a piece of land planted with grapes for making wine
waterfront part of a town near a sea or ocean
✓**winery** a factory that makes wine

48

3 GUESS THE STORY

Watch the video with the sound off. Where do you think the couple goes first?

1) Sausalito   2) The Napa Valley   3) Muir Woods

 *Watch the video*

4 GET THE PICTURE

What places does the car-rental agent talk about? Circle them.
Then compare with a partner.

(The Napa Valley)   Oakland   Alcatraz Island

Sausalito   Muir Woods   The Golden Gate Bridge

5 WATCH FOR DETAILS

Why should the Changs go to the places below? Complete the sentences.
Then compare with a partner.

1) The *wineries* and .... there are some of the most famous in California.

2) It's a fascinating little .... just across the ....

3) It's right on the ...., and there's a wonderful view of .... across the ....

4) It's a beautiful redwood ....

6 COMPLETE THE STORY

Complete the paragraph below. Choose words from the list. Then compare with a partner.

Golden Gate	hungry	the Napa Valley	Sausalito	week
✓Honolulu	Muir Woods	rent	waterfront	wineries

The Changs arrive in San Francisco from .... *Honolulu* .... They ....
a car at the airport for one .... because they plan to visit friends in
.... The rental agent tells them about the famous ....
there. They decide to drive across the .... Bridge and have lunch in
.... on the way.

Follow-up

7 SAN FRANCISCO

Group work Imagine you have two days in San Francisco. Plan your itinerary.

1) Decide which places you will go to each day.
2) Decide if you need a car.

DAY 1	DAY 2
....	....
....	....
....	....

Ghirardelli Square

Golden Gate Park

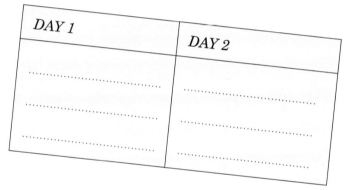

Fisherman's Wharf

Muir Woods

Chinatown

Sausalito

8 YOUR CITY

A Group work Now imagine the Changs are visiting your city. Plan their itinerary. Give at least six suggestions like this:

A: First, I think they should drive to . . .
B: Yes, and they should also go to . . .

B Class activity Share your information with the class.

Language close-up

9 WHAT DID THEY SAY?

Watch the video and complete the conversation. Then practice it.

The Changs are at the car-rental agency at the airport.

Ken: Good .... *morning* .... May I ....*help*..... you?

Mr. Chang: Yes, we're .... to pick up a ....

Ken: Do you .... a reservation?

Mr. Chang: Yes. The .... is Chang.

Ken: OK, Chang, Chang. Here it is, Mr. Chang.
                .... in advance. .... here and here.
                And that's for one .... then?

Mr. Chang: That's .... One week.

Ken: Are you .... in San Francisco?

Mrs. Chang: No, we're .... to visit ....
                in the Napa Valley.

Ken: Oh, Napa Valley. That's one of my ....
                places. The wineries and .... there are some
                of the most .... in California.

---

10 SHOULD *AND* SHOULDN'T *Giving advice*

A Complete these sentences with **should** or **shouldn't**. Then
compare with a partner

1) When you visit a foreign country, you .... *should* .... learn
   a few words of the local language.
2) You .... find out about the weather before you travel.
3) You .... carry a lot of cash when you travel.
4) You .... talk to a travel agent about interesting
   places to visit.
5) You .... be afraid to ask local people questions.

B *Pair work* Give advice for things visitors to your city should or
shouldn't do. Write three suggestions in each column.

They should . . .	They shouldn't . . .
1)	1) ....
2)	2) ....
3)	3) ....

Feeling bad

1 CULTURE

In the United States and Canada, people spend more on health care than in other parts of the world. In drugstores, people buy over-the-counter drugs for colds, coughs, and sore throats. In health-food stores, they buy vitamins and natural foods. Home remedies for common illnesses such as colds and sore throats are also popular.

Do you take vitamins or other food supplements?
Do you have health-food stores in your country? What do they sell?

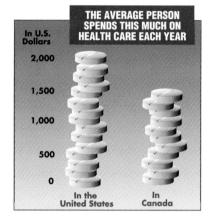

THE AVERAGE PERSON SPENDS THIS MUCH ON HEALTH CARE EACH YEAR

In U.S. Dollars

2,000
1,500
1,000
500
0

In the United States   In Canada

2 VOCABULARY Cold remedies

Pair work Put the remedies in the chart. Can you add two more to each category?

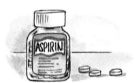

aspirin

chicken soup

cough medicine

garlic juice

ginseng tea

tea with lemon

Home remedies		Over-the-counter drugs	
chicken soup	....	....	....
....	....	....	....
....	....	....	....

52

3 GUESS THE STORY

Watch the video with the sound off. Answer these questions.

What's the man's problem?
Which remedies in Exercise 2 do you think his co-workers suggest?

 Watch the video

4 GET THE PICTURE

Check (✓) the correct answers. Compare them with a partner.

1) Sandy offers Steve
   ☐ something she made.
   ☐ something from the drugstore.
   ☐ something from a health-food store.

2) Jim offers Steve
   ☐ something he bought.
   ☐ something his mother makes for him.
   ☐ something from a health-food store.

3) Rebecca says Steve should
   ☐ see the doctor.
   ☐ take some more medicine.
   ☐ go out to lunch.

5 WATCH FOR DETAILS

Check (✓) all correct answers. Then compare with a partner.

1) Sandy says her remedy
   ☐ tastes bad.
   ☐ contains ginseng.
   ☐ makes you sleepy.

2) Jim says his remedy
   ☐ is great for a cold.
   ☐ makes you sleepy.
   ☐ has garlic, onions, and carrots in it.

3) Rebecca says her remedy
   ☐ is the best cure of all.
   ☐ can be made at home.
   ☐ mixes with water.

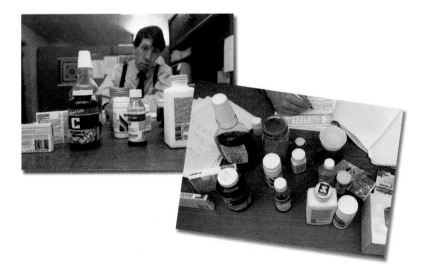

53

6 WHAT'S YOUR OPINION?

Pair work Answer these questions.

1) Which remedy does Steve like best?
2) Which remedy do you think is best for Steve's cold?
3) Do you think Steve should be at work today?

 *Follow-up*

7 HEALTH PROBLEMS

A *Group work* What do you do for these problems? Can you add two more remedies for each? Compare around the class. Who has the best remedies?

1) a bad cold
It's a good idea to
stay in bed and rest.
Try some . . .
....
....

2) a cough
You should drink hot
tea.
It's important to . . .
....
....

3) a headache
Take some aspirin.
It's helpful to . . .
....
....

4) a backache
You should lie on the
floor.
Get some . . .
....
....

B *Pair work* Take turns playing the role of Steve. Your partner will give you advice.

A: How do you feel?
B: Not too good. I've got . . .
A: That's too bad. Listen. I've got the perfect cure . . .

C Do you need advice for a problem of your own? Have a similar conversation, using personal information.

Language close-up

8 WHAT DID THEY SAY?

Watch the video and complete the conversation. Then practice it.

Steve is at work with a bad cold when Sandy comes in.

Sandy: How are those .....*papers*..... coming for this
...........*afternoon*........... , Steve?

Steve: .... finished.

Sandy: Do you .... have that .... ?

Steve: Yeah, ... still pretty .... , Sandy.

Sandy: Listen, I've .... just the .... for you. Just a
.... Here.

Steve: What's .... ?

Sandy: It's .... I picked up at the ....-food
store. You just mix it with .... water and .... it.

Steve: But .... is it?

Sandy: I'm not really .... I think it .... ginseng in it or
something .... that. Try it.

Steve: Are you sure it .... ?

Sandy: Of .... it does.

Steve: Well, ... , Sandy. That's really .... Maybe later.

---

9 REQUESTS AND SUGGESTIONS

A Complete the conversations with **may** or **could** to make
requests and **should**, **try**, or **suggest** to give suggestions.
Then compare and practice with a partner.

1) *At the office*

A: Here's the perfect cold medicine: garlic juice, onions,
and carrots. You .....*should*..... drink a cup every two hours.

B: But I don't like carrots.

A: Well, then I .... an old-fashioned bowl of chicken
soup! And .... to get some rest, too.

2) *At a pharmacy*

A: .... I help you?

B: Yes. .... I have something good for a cold? It's a bad one.

A: Yes. I have these pills. They're a little strong. Just don't drive after
you take them.

B: Hmm . . . I drive to work. .... I have something else?

A: Well, ... these other pills then. They won't make you sleepy.

B *Pair work* Act out the conversations. The first time, act them out as is.
The second time, change the problems and the remedies.

55

Documentary 4
At the Mall of America

Preview

1 CULTURE

The Mall of America is the largest shopping and entertainment mall in the United States. It takes up 4.2 million square feet (or 390,000 square meters) of space. In addition to four major department stores, you can find almost 400 other stores, an entertainment park with 50 rides, over 30 restaurants, a movie theater with 14 screens, and numerous live music clubs. Built in 1990, the mall is still very new. The original idea for the mall came from the Triple Five Corporation, a Canadian company that built the largest shopping mall in the world in West Edmonton, Alberta.

Are shopping malls popular in your country?
What do you think are the advantages of shopping at a mall?
  The disadvantages?

Watch the video

2 GET THE PICTURE

Check (✓) the correct answers. Then compare with a partner.

1) The Mall of America is in
   ☐ Bloomington, Indiana.
   ✓ Bloomington, Minnesota.

2) The mall has
   ☐ hundreds of stores.
   ☐ thousands of stores.

3) There are
   ☐ 14 cinemas.
   ☐ 40 cinemas.

4) There are more than
   ☐ 14 places to eat.
   ☐ 40 places to eat.

5) The name of the amusement park is
   ☐ Camp Winnie.
   ☐ Camp Snoopy.

56

3 WATCH FOR DETAILS

What did these people do at the mall? Check (✓) all true answers. Then compare with a partner.

1) ☐ She went to Camp Snoopy.
   ☐ She bought some shoes.
   ☐ She ate lunch.

2) ☐ They went on rides.
   ☐ They looked in stores.
   ☐ They ate lunch.

3) ☐ They listened to music.
   ☐ They bought some tapes.
   ☐ They went to Camp Snoopy.

4 WHAT THE SHOPPERS SAY

How did these people answer the reporter's questions? Fill in the blanks. Then compare with a partner.

1) What do you think people should do first?

2) What would you recommend for visitors from another country?

3) Can you describe the Mall of America in one word?

Wear .... shoes.

Come here if there's anything .... you're looking for.

....

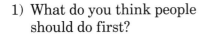

Follow-up

5 WHAT'S YOUR OPINION?

Pair work Answer these questions.

1) Do you like shopping malls?
2) How would you describe the Mall of America?
3) What places would you like to visit at the mall?

13 At the state fair

1 CULTURE

In rural areas of the United States and Canada, where farming is important, a state or county fair is a popular summer event. At the fair, farmers show their fruits and vegetables, their best animals, and their new equipment. There are competitions such as horseback riding and rodeos. People sell paintings and handmade products such as pottery. There are rides and games for the entire family. And there are always lots of things to eat. For young children, a day at the fair is one of the happiest days of the year.

Do you have fairs in your country? What kind? What can you do and see there?

Where can families go in your country to have fun together?

2 VOCABULARY At a state fair

Pair work Here are some things you can do at a state fair. Write the activities under the pictures.

eat corn on the cob   ride a horse   ride on a roller coaster
eat ice cream   ride on a merry-go-round   ✓win a prize

1) *win a prize*

2) ....

3) ....

4) ....

5) ....

6) ....

58

3 GUESS THE STORY

Who do you think wins the prize? Check (✓) your answer.

☐ Rick   ☐ Betsy   ☐ Nancy

 Watch the video

4 GET THE PICTURE

What did each group of people do? Check (✓) all correct answers.
Then compare with a partner.

	Liz and Steve	Nancy, Betsy, and Rick	Paul and Cynthia
1) won a prize	☐	✓	☐
2) had some ice cream	☐	☐	☐
3) ate some corn on the cob	☐	☐	☐
4) went on a ride	☐	☐	☐
5) had some lunch	☐	☐	☐

5 WATCH FOR DETAILS

A List the things to do, eat, and see at a state fair. Then combine
answers as a class and complete the chart.

Things to do	Things to eat	Things to see
ride a horse		

B Which of these things have you done? Check (✓) them.
Then compare with a partner.

Follow-up

6 *A DAY AT THE FAIR*

A *Group work* Plan a day at the state fair in the video. Agree on five things to do and see.

1) ....
2) ....
3) ....
4) ....
5) ....

B *Pair work* Order lunch at the state fair. One student will play the waiter or waitress.

A: May I take your order, please?
B: . . .
A: Would you like anything else?
B: . . .
A: And would you like anything to drink?
B: . . .

7 YOUR COUNTRY

A *Group work* What can you do at a fair in your country? Make a list.

Things to do	Things to eat	Things to see
....	....	....
....	....	....
....	....	....
....	....	....

B Which things are your favorite? Check (✓) at least three. Then have conversations like this:

A: I like to go on rides.
B: I like to play games and try to win prizes.

C In the United States, corn on the cob is very popular. What foods are popular where you're from?

Language close-up

8 *WHAT DID THEY SAY?*

Watch the video and complete the conversations. Then practice them.

Some people are enjoying a day at the state fair.

1) Vendor: Hey, this is the ....*place*....... ! Get your fresh corn on
   the .... here! Fresh, ...-roasted ....
   on the cob! . . . What .... you like?

   Steve: I'll .... one of .... , please.

   Vendor: Coming .... What about .... ? Would you
   .... one, too?

   Liz: Not right .... , thank you. I'm not ....

   Steve: Maybe you .... give us another .... anyway!

   Vendor: Sure.

2) Nancy: Oh, he is *so* .... !

   Rick: Yeah, but that .... a lot of .... Now let's .... a
   place to ....

   Betsy: How about over .... ? There's a ....
   where we can .... down, too. My .... are tired.

   Waitress: Hi! .... I take your .... ?

   Betsy: Yeah, I .... I'll have a hot .... and a small ....
   of french fries.

   Waitress: Would you .... anything to .... ?

   Betsy: I'll have a .... diet cola.

   Waitress: OK. And .... can I .... for you?

   Nancy: I guess .... like the .... plate and a cup of .... , please.

---

9 WOULD *AND* WILL *Ordering food*

A Rewrite these questions using **Would you like . . . ?**
Then compare with a partner.

1) What do you want to eat?
   What would you like to eat?

2) Do you want french fries with that?

   ....

3) Do you want dessert?

   ....

4) Do you want anything to drink?

   ....

B *Pair work* Now answer the questions with **I'll have . . .**

A: What would you like to eat?
B: I'll have . . .

14 Around the World: the game show

1 CULTURE

One of the most popular TV programs in the United States and Canada is the game show. In most game shows, players test their knowledge on different subjects, and the questions are sometimes difficult. But there are also game shows that are games of chance. The winner must be lucky, but doesn't have to be smart. And there are even dating "game shows." The prize isn't money, but a chance to meet someone new!

Do you have game shows on TV in your country?
What kinds of game shows are popular?

POPULAR TV

JEOPARDY
A Game of Knowledge
Love Connection
A Dating Game
Wheel of Fortune
A Game of Chance

GAME SHOWS
IN THE U.S.

2 GUESS THE FACTS

Pair work How good is your geography?
Check the correct answers.

1) Which is longer?
   ☐ the Nile River
   ☐ the Amazon River

2) Which is higher?
   ☐ Mt. McKinley
   ☐ Mt. Kilimanjaro

3) Which country is called the "island continent"?
   ☐ New Zealand
   ☐ Australia

the Amazon River

the Nile River

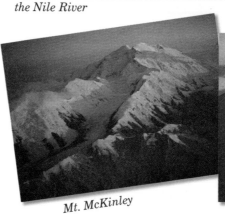

Mt. McKinley

Mt. Kilimanjaro

4) What's the largest desert in Asia?
   ☐ the Great Indian desert
   ☐ the Gobi desert

Los Angeles

Mexico City

5) Which is the largest city in North America?
   ☐ Los Angeles
   ☐ Mexico City

6) Where is Angel Falls, the world's highest waterfall?
   ☐ Brazil
   ☐ Venezuela

Angel Falls

 **Watch the video**

3 CHECK THE FACTS

Now correct your answers to Exercise 2. Did you guess the facts correctly? Compare with a partner.

4 WATCH FOR DETAILS

Check (✓) the correct answers. Then compare with a partner.

1) Marlene is from
   ☐ Seattle, Washington.
   ☐ Washington, D.C.

2) Marlene is a
   ☐ computer programmer.
   ☐ computer engineer.

3) Jack is from
   ☐ Cambridge, Massachusetts.
   ☐ Boston, Massachusetts.

4) Jack is a
   ☐ high school teacher.
   ☐ college teacher.

5) Kathy is from
   ☐ Vero Beach, Florida.
   ☐ Miami Beach, Florida.

6) Kathy is an
   ☐ actress.
   ☐ accountant.

5 WHO WINS THE GAME?

A What is each person's score at the end of the game? Write the
number. Then compare with a partner.

Marlene .... Jack .... Kathy ....

B Is the winner happy with the prize? Why or why not?

Follow-up

6 AROUND THE WORLD

A *Group work* Write questions for the game "Around the World."
Write three questions for each category in the chart. Give one question
25 points, one question 50 points, and one question 75 points. (You can
also add categories of your own.)

Deserts and mountains	*Oceans and islands*
....	....
....	....
....	....
Rivers and waterfalls	*Cities and countries*
....	....
....	....
....	....

B *Class activity* Now play "Around the World." Half the class
is in Group A. The other half is in Group B.

Group A: Choose one student to be the game-show host.

Group B: Take turns choosing a category for 25, 50, or 75 points.
Then answer the host's questions. Play for five minutes.

Ask questions like this:

A: Are you ready?
B: Yes, I'll try (*name of category*) for 25 points.
A: OK. (*Asks question.*)
B: (*Answers question.*)
A: That's right! **or** Sorry. That's not correct.

Now change roles. Group B chooses a host and Group A
answers questions. Play for five more minutes. Which group
wins the game?

Language close-up

7 WHAT DID THEY SAY?

Watch the video and complete the conversation. Then practice it.

Marlene, Jack, and Kathy are about to begin playing "Around the World."

Announcer: And now it's .....*time*.... to play "Around the .....*World*..... "
with your host, Johnny Traveler.

Johnny: .... and gentlemen, ... to
"Around the World," the .... show about world
.... And now, let's .... our players.

Announcer: A .... engineer from .... ,
Washington, Marlene Miller! A high ....
teacher from .... , Massachusetts, Jack
Richardson! And from Vero Beach, Florida, an
.... , Kathy Hernandez!

Johnny: .... to "Around the World." And now, let's
.... our game. Our categories are ....
and Mountains, ... and Waterfalls, Oceans and
.... , Cities and .... Marlene, please begin.

8 COMPARISONS WITH ADJECTIVES

A Write questions using the comparative or superlative form of each
adjective in parentheses. Then add three questions of your own.

1) city: New York – Tokyo? (cold)
   Which city is colder, New York or Tokyo?

2) planet: Earth – Saturn – Mars? (big)
   ....

3) plane: the Concorde – a 747? (fast)
   ....

4) building: the World Trade Center – the Empire
   State Building? (old)
   ....

5) country: Brazil – Canada – Argentina? (large)
   ....

6) ....

7) ....

8) ....

New York is colder!

B *Pair work* Take turns asking and answering the questions.
Who answered the most questions correctly?

15 May I speak to Cathy?

Preview

1 CULTURE

In the United States and Canada, people like to talk on the telephone. In many places, the cost of a local call is fixed. You can talk for five minutes or two hours for the same price. The telephone is now very convenient because of new technology. Here are some examples:

- *Call waiting* – You can answer a second call when you are on the telephone.
- *Call forwarding* – You can receive telephone calls at a different phone number.
- *Answering machines* – You don't miss calls when you're busy or not at home.
- *Cellular phones* – You can make and receive telephone calls in your car.
- *Two telephone lines on one phone* – Different rings tell you who the call is for.

How much time do you spend on the telephone each day?
What kinds of new technology are common in your country?
  Which do you like best?

2 VOCABULARY *Telephone expressions*

A *Pair work* Match.

.....c..... 1) Cathy's not here right now.
.... 2) May I speak to Cathy?
.... 3) She's not in just now.
.... 4) Will she be back soon?
.... 5) Could you tell her that Kevin called?
.... 6) Is she coming back soon?
.... 7) Is Cathy home?
.... 8) Could you just tell her to call me?

a) Asking to speak to someone
b) Leaving a message
c) Saying someone is out
d) Asking for information about someone

B Can you add three other telephone expressions?

1) ....

2) ....

3) ....

3 GUESS THE STORY

Watch the first two minutes of the video with the sound off.
What do you think these people are saying? Write one sentence from
Exercise 2 in each balloon.

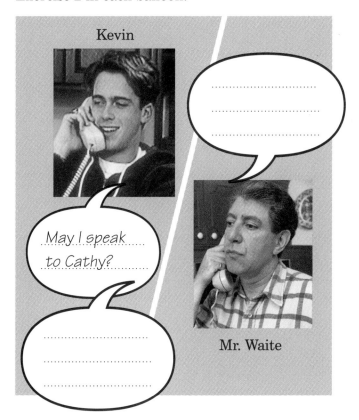

Kevin

Mr. Waite

May I speak
to Cathy?

Mr. Waite

Jenny

Watch the video

4 GET THE PICTURE

A Put the phone calls in order. Number them from 1 to 3. Then compare with a partner.

Kevin   Rachel   Jenny

B Complete the telephone messages for Cathy. Fill in the names of the callers
and check the correct messages. Then compare with a partner.

1) .... called.
  ☐ will call Cathy back
  ☐ wants Cathy to call

2) .... called.
  ☐ will call Cathy back
  ☐ wants Cathy to call

3) .... called.
  ☐ will call Cathy back
  ☐ wants Cathy to call

5 TELEPHONE ETIQUETTE

A When you make a phone call, it's polite to give your name. What does each person say when Mr. Waite answers the phone? Fill in the balloons. Then compare with a partner.

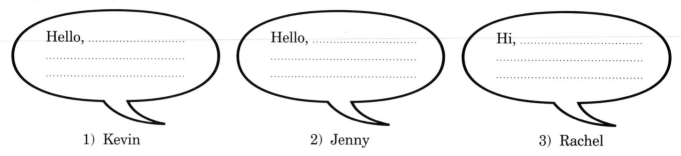

1) Kevin   2) Jenny   3) Rachel

B *Pair work* Who do you think is the most polite? Why?

6 WHAT'S YOUR OPINION?

Pair work Look at the culture preview again. Which telephone conveniences do you think Mr. Waite needs? Give each a number from 1 to 5 (1 = most useful).

Follow-up

7 FINISH THE STORY

A *Pair work* What do you think Mr. Waite says to his boss? What do you think the urgent call was about? Write a possible telephone conversation.

Start like this:

Mr. Waite: John speaking.
Boss: I'm very sorry to bother you, John. I hope it's not a problem.
Mr. Waite: Oh no, no! Uh, no problem! No problem at all!
Boss: I'm calling because . . .
Mr. Waite: . . .

B *Class activity* Practice your conversations in front of the class. Who has the best conversation?

Language close-up

8 WHAT DID THEY SAY?

Watch the video and complete the conversations. Then practice them.

Cathy's father is home alone when the phone rings.

1) Mr. Waite: Hello?
   Kevin: Hello, ...*may*... I speak ...*to*... Cathy?
   Mr. Waite: I'm .... She's not .... just now.
   Kevin: Is she .... back soon?
   Mr. Waite: Uh, ... , I think ....
   Kevin: Well, ... you tell .... that
   Kevin .... and that I'll call .... later?
   Mr. Waite: .... , Kevin.
   Kevin: .... you. Good-bye.
   Mr. Waite: Bye.

2) Mr. Waite: Hello?
   Jenny: .... , Mr. Waite. .... is Jenny. Is
   Cathy .... ?
   Mr. Waite: Oh, hi, Jenny. No, Cathy's .... here
   right ....
   Jenny: .... she be .... soon?
   Mr. Waite: Uh, I'm not .... Would you ....
   to leave a .... ?
   Jenny: Well, ... you just .... her to call ....
   when she .... in?
   Mr. Waite: Sure, ... tell her. .... , Jenny.
   Jenny: Bye, ... Waite.

3) Mr. Waite: Hello?
   Rachel: .... , this is Rachel. .... Cathy home?
   Mr. Waite: Uh, no, she's .... , Rachel. .... you like
   her to .... you .... she comes .... ?
   Rachel: Yes, ... She has my ....
   Mr. Waite: I'll .... her, Rachel. Bye.
   Rachel: Bye.

9 REQUESTS WITH TELL AND ASK

Pair work Practice the conversations in Exercise 8 again.
This time use your own information and make requests with
ask or **tell** like this:

Would you tell Cathy the party is at Kevin's house?
Could you ask Cathy to meet us at Burger Heaven at 2:00?

69

 **A whole new Marty**

1 CULTURE

Self-improvement is an important part of Canadian and American cultures. Many people believe that life will be better for them if they change their appearance in some way. Magazines and newspapers often have advertisements for exercise machines, vitamins, skin and hair products, and courses on self-improvement. Among young people, a good appearance is usually important, and so is the ability to make friends easily.

Is self-improvement an important part of your culture?
Do you want to change anything about yourself?

3 Steps to a Better You

1 Exercise bicycle $119.95

2 Self-help book $19.95 *I Love Me*

3 Super vitamins $39.95

TO ORDER, CALL 800-555-3210

2 VOCABULARY Verb and noun pairs

Pair work Choose a verb from the list to go with each word or phrase.
(Some items have more than one answer.)

| buy | cut | gain | ✓improve | make |
| ✓change | do | get | lose | meet |

1) *change or improve* .... my appearance
2) .... more people
3) .... more friends
4) .... weight
5) .... more exercise
6) .... some new clothes
7) .... my hairstyle
8) .... my hair
9) .... in shape
10) .... confidence

3 GUESS THE STORY

Watch the first minute of the video with the sound off.
Check (✓) the phrases you think describe each person.

	Marty	John
1) looks unhappy	☐	☐
2) is popular with girls	☐	☐
3) dresses well	☐	☐
4) has trouble with a calculus problem	☐	☐

Marty

John

 **Watch the video**

4 GET THE PICTURE

A Check your answers to Exercise 3. Did you guess correctly?

B Check (✓) **True** or **False**. Correct the false statements. Then compare with a partner.

Marty

John

Michelle

	True	*False*	
1) John asks Marty for help with his schoolwork.	☐	☐	....
2) Michelle doesn't know Marty.	☐	☐	....
3) Michelle and John decide to study calculus together.	☐	☐	....
4) John thinks Marty should be more outgoing.	☐	☐	....
5) Michelle recognizes Marty in the cafeteria.	☐	☐	....
6) Marty is too busy to study with Michelle.	☐	☐	....

5 WATCH FOR DETAILS

Check (✓) the things Marty does to improve his appearance.

☐ He lifts weights.

☐ He gets a haircut.

☐ He changes his diet.

☐ He buys new clothes.

☐ He shaves.

☐ He takes vitamins.

Follow-up

6 WHAT HAPPENED?

A Write the story in your own words.

1) *John and Marty were in the library.*

2) ....

3) ....

4) ....

5) ....

6) ....

B *Pair work* Now share your description of what happened with a partner. How are your stories different?

7 GOOD ADVICE

What advice would you give to these people? Think of as many things as you can for each person.

1) Maria has trouble meeting boys.
2) Tina has trouble with math.
3) Tony is shy.
4) Karen wants to get in shape.

He could . . .
She should . . .
It's important/helpful/useful/a good idea to . . .

Language close-up

8 WHAT DID THEY SAY?

Watch the video and complete the conversation. Then practice it.

John and Marty are in the library when Michelle comes by.

John: I'm just ....*terrible*.... at calculus. I don't ....
anything in this ....

Marty: I .... what you .... It is a .... course.

John: Did you .... out the answer to this .... ?

Marty: That's in Chapter 11. I .... that .... week. Let's see.

Michelle: Hi, John. I .... you're .... on calculus.

John: Oh, hi, Michelle. Yes, I .... Michelle, you .... Marty,
.... you?

Michelle: Yeah, hi, Marty. Say, John, I've got a .... of
.... about Chapter 12. Do you want to
.... together?

John: Well, uh, actually, I'm .... on Chapter 11, but Marty
.... is working on Chapter 12.

Michelle: Oh, that's OK. Actually, I've .... go to class
.... now. See you ....

John: OK, Michelle. ....

9 DESCRIBING CHANGES

A Complete the sentences with the correct form of each word.
Then compare with a partner.

busy   buy   change   drive
long   paint   start   wear

1) I .... glasses now.

2) I don't .... to work anymore. I take the bus.

3) I haven't cut my hair in four months. It's .... than before.

4) I got a promotion at work recently. I'm much .... now.

5) I .... my bedroom blue last weekend.

6) I .... a new computer course last week.

7) I've .... a dog.

8) I've .... my hairstyle.

B Now write four similar sentences about yourself and read them to your partner.
Who has changed more in the past year?

1) ....   3) ....

2) ....   4) ....

Documentary 5
What is American food?

Preview

1 CULTURE

Many people think American food is just hot dogs and pizza. Of course, these things are popular, but even in small towns in the United States, you can find Chinese, Italian, and Mexican restaurants. In many places there are Japanese, Thai, and German restaurants. The United States is a country of immigrants, and there are as many kinds of food as there are people from different backgrounds.

What foods are typical of your country or region?
What is your favorite food?

Watch the video

2 GET THE PICTURE

In the video, in what kind of restaurant can you find these foods?
Write **CA** for California style, **A** for American, **C** for Chinese,
or **G** for German.

1) bratwurst

2) Caesar salad

3) a hamburger

4) Kung-pao chicken

5) pasta

6) pork Szechwan

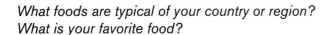

3 WATCH FOR DETAILS

Match the people with what they ate. Choose foods
from the list. Then compare with a partner.

Bavarian goulash	Caesar salad	German potato salad	pasta
bratwurst	chicken salad	Kung-pao chicken	pork Szechwan

1) ....

2) ....

3) ....

4) ....

5) ....

6) ....

4 IT'S ALL AMERICAN FOOD

Answer the questions. Then compare with a partner.

1) California-style restaurants are famous for
   their interesting use of
   ☐ fresh fish.
   ☐ pasta.
   ☑ fresh fruits and vegetables.

2) The Chinese restaurant has
   ☐ food with live music.
   ☐ a self-service buffet.
   ☐ vegetarian food.

3) In the German restaurant people can
   ☐ listen to music and eat.
   ☐ cook their own food.
   ☐ order a hamburger.

4) Most people in the video think typical
   American food is
   ☐ steak.
   ☐ a hamburger and french fries.
   ☐ barbecue.

 **Follow-up**

5 HOW ABOUT YOU?

Group work Answer these questions.

1) What does the reporter say American food is?
   What is American food to you?
2) How often do you eat out in restaurants?

3) What's your favorite kind of restaurant?
4) What do you usually order?
5) What's your favorite American food?

Acknowledgments

Illustrators

Adventure House 6 (*top*), 12 (*top*), 16, 18, 26 (*top*), 34 (*all*), 37, 48 (*top*), 52 (*top*), 62, 70

Brian Battles 12 (*bottom*), 14 (*bottom*)

Keith Bendis 2, 8, 10, 26 (*bottom*), 30, 42, 54, 66, 71

Mark Kaufman 48 (*bottom*), 58 (*top*)

Wally Neibart 4, 14 (*top*), 22 (*top*), 27, 36, 52 (*bottom*), 58 (*bottom*), 65

Andrew Toos 6 (*bottom*), 22 (*bottom*), 28, 39, 40, 44, 55, 61

Sam Viviano 24

Photographic Credits

49 (*top left*) © Bill Dean

62 (*clockwise from top left*) © Richard Steedman/The Stock Market; © Claudia Parks/The Stock Market; © Harvey Lloyd/The Stock Market; © Tom Bean/ The Stock Market

63 (*top; clockwise from top left*) © Pete Saloutos/The Stock Market; © Nigel Atherton/Tony Stone Worldwide; © Rob Crandall/Stock Boston

All other photographs by Rick Armstrong and John Hruska

Author's Acknowledgments

A great number of people assisted in the development of both the original *Interchange* Video 1 and *New Interchange* Video 1. Particular thanks go to the following:

The **reviewers** for their helpful suggestions:

Valerie A. Benson, Julie Dyson, Dorien Grunbaum, Cynthia Hall Kouré, Mark Kunce, Peter Mallett, Pamela Rogerson-Revell, Chuck Sandy, and Jody Simmons.

The **students** and **teachers** in the following schools and institutes who pilot-tested the Video or the Video Activity Book; their valuable comments and suggestions helped shape the content of the entire program:

Athenée Français, Tokyo, Japan; **Centro Cultural Brasil-Estados Unidos**, Belém, Brazil; **Eurocentres**, Virginia, U.S.A.; **Fairmont State College**, West Virginia, U.S.A.; **Hakodate Daigaku**, Hokkaido, Japan; **Hirosaki Gakuin Daigaku**, Aomori, Japan; **Hiroshima Shudo Daigaku**, Hiroshima, Japan; **Hokkaido Daigaku, Institute of Language and Cultural Studies**, Hokkaido, Japan; **The Institute Meguro**, Tokyo, Japan; **Instituto Brasil-Estados Unidos**, Rio de Janeiro, Brazil; **Instituto Cultural de Idiomas**, Caxias do Sul, Brazil; **Musashino Joshi Daigaku**, Tokyo, Japan; **Nagasaki Gaigo Tanki Daigaku**, Nagasaki, Japan; **New Cida**, Tokyo, Japan; **Parco-ILC English School**, Chiba, Japan; **Pegasus Language Services**, Tokyo, Japan; **Poole Gakuin Tanki Daigaku**, Hyogo, Japan; **Seinan Gakuin Daigaku**, Fukuoka, Japan;

Shukugawa Joshi Tanki Daigaku, Hyogo, Japan; **Tokai Daigaku**, Kanagawa, Japan; **YMCA Business School**, Kanagawa, Japan; and **Yokohama YMCA**, Kanagawa, Japan.

The **editorial** and **production** team on the original or revised classroom video and the accompanying print materials:

Sarah Almy, Suzette André, John Borrelli, Will Capel, Mary Carson, Karen Davy, Andrew Gitzy, Deborah Goldblatt, Deborah Gordon, Stephanie Karras, James Morgan, Kathy Niemczyk, Chuck Sandy, Kathleen Schultz, Ellen Shaw, and Mary Vaughn.

The **editorial** and **production** team on *New Interchange* Level One: Suzette André, Sylvia P. Bloch, John Borrelli, Mary Carson, Natalie Nordby Chen, Karen Davy, Randee Falk, Andrew Gitzy, Pauline Ireland, Penny Laporte, Kathy Niemczyk, Kathleen Schultz, Rosie Stamp, and Mary Vaughn.

And Cambridge University Press **staff** and **advisors**: Carlos Barbisan, Kate Cory-Wright, Riitta da Costa, Peter Davison, Stephen Dawson, Peter Donovan, Cecilia Gómez, Colin Hayes, Thares Keeree, Jinsook Kim, Koen Van Landeghem, Carine Mitchell, Sabina Sahni, Helen Sandiford, Dan Schulte, Ian Sutherland, Chris White, and Ellen Zlotnick.

And a special thanks to the video producer, Master Communications Group.